Grade 3

Building
Fluency
Through Practice & Performance

Written and Compiled by

Timothy Rasinski and Lorraine Griffith

SHELL EDUCATION

Editor
Jodene Lynn Smith, M.A.

Assistant Editor
Katie Das

Editorial Director
Dona Herweck Rice

Editor-in-Chief
Sharon Coan, M.S.Ed.

Editorial Manager
Gisela Lee, M.A.

Creative Director
Lee Aucoin

Illustration Manager/Designer
Timothy J. Bradley

Artist
Timothy J. Bradley

Print Production
Robin Erickson

Publisher
Corinne Burton, M.A.Ed

All songs performed by An Old Folkie and the Turkey Creek Minstrels: Stephen Griffith (lead male vocals and guitar), Jen Whipple (lead female vocalist), Kate Brown Walters (harmonies), Julie Eargle, Gary Frink, Kevin Auman, Betty Jackson, Ben Thompson, and Lorraine Griffith (lead vocal on My Old Kentucky Home), Ben Thompson (Lead Picker), Julie Eargle (Rhythm Guitar), Gary Frink (Bass).

All recordings produced by Kevin Auman, Stephen Griffith, and Gary Frink. Audio production and engineering by Kevin Auman. Recorded at Perelandra Studio, Asheville, NC. All songs and tunes are in the public domain. Recordings copyright © 2008, Stephen Griffith.

Shell Education
5301 Oceanus Drive
Huntington Beach, CA 92649-1030
http://www.shelleducation.com
ISBN 978-1-4258-0443-5
© 2008 Shell Educational Publishing, Inc.
Reprinted 2010

Table of Contents

Table of Contents *(cont.)*

Foreword

By Timothy Rasinski

We are so glad you have chosen this book. As an elementary teacher or a teacher working with children who struggle to learn, reading is central to your curriculum. This book provides you with a wealth of materials for developing a key but often neglected aspect of the elementary reading curriculum—reading fluency. This book also gives you the materials to make reading a fun, engaging, varied, and authentic activity for your students.

Fluency consists of two critical components: automaticity in word recognition and expressive or prosodic reading (Rasinski 2003). Automaticity refers to the ability to read words in text so effortlessly that readers can direct their limited cognitive resources away from word recognition and use those resources for what really matters in reading— making meaning or comprehension. Expressive or prosodic reading refers to the melodic part of reading in which the readers create meaning with their voices (in silent or oral reading). The meaning in a text is not only carried by the words, but also by the way in which the words are read—with expression, appropriate phrasing and varied pace, emphasis on particular words, through dramatic pauses, and more.

In most current fluency programs, automaticity is the primary aim (Rasinski 2006). Readers are asked to repeatedly read a great deal of informational text with the emphasis on reading it quickly because reading rate is a measure of automaticity. Prosodic reading is generally given second-tier status at best in such programs. Informational text does not lend itself easily to expressive reading, and reading a text quickly does not allow much opportunity for students to work using expression while reading.

Our approach to fluency, the one deeply embedded in this book, acknowledges that guided repeated reading, or rehearsal, is key to the development of automaticity. However, the aim of rehearsal should not only be speed (reading rate will increase through practice with or without explicit instruction in or emphasis on speed-reading); rather, the emphasis of the rehearsal is to bring the author's voice to life. This is prosody or expressive reading. In order to do this, you need texts that have a strong sense of voice. That is what this book consists of—passages of a variety of genres that have voice and are meant to be read orally, usually performed for an audience. To deliver a satisfying performance, readers need to read with accuracy, automaticity, and meaningful expression.

This book is, at its core, a collection of poems, songs, scripts, and other materials appropriate for young readers that tend to be strongly connected to our cultural heritage. Thus, the materials in this book offer you a wonderful opportunity to develop the cultural literacy and cultural appreciation that define who we are as an English-speaking people. Moreover, the diversity of genres in this book, going beyond the narratives and informational texts that currently tend to dominate elementary reading curricula, provides you with a much richer and varied palette of texts from which to create your overall reading program (Rasinski, in press).

Foreword (cont.)

We provide suggestions in the following section on how to use the passages in the book. However, the actual use of this wonderful material is really up to you. We suggest that you select passages that are relevant to what you may be studying or that are related to current events or dates. Assign selections to individuals or groups of students. Feel free to assign the same passage to more than one individual or group. Allow students to practice or rehearse the passages, with a focus on reading the selection orally with appropriate expression and meaning. Given the importance of repeated readings, we feel that the rehearsal time should take several days. While students rehearse, be sure to model expressive reading, listen, provide formative feedback and encouragement to students, and arrange a time for students to perform their selections to the rest of the class or another audience.

The guided or reading practice that is part of the rehearsal process is essential to students' reading development. Research has shown that guided rehearsal leads to substantial improvements in students' reading fluency and comprehension (Chard, Vaughn, & Tyler 2002; Dowhower 1987, 1994; Kuhn & Stahl 2000; Rasinski & Hoffman 2003; Samuels 1979). With Building Fluency Through Practice and Performance, students are exposed to authentic and meaningful material, and they have the chance to perform for an authentic audience. Through this process, students learn greater content, appreciate genres beyond narration (stories) and exposition (informational texts), and develop a sense of confidence in themselves as readers and learners that is essential to their ultimate success in school and in life (Griffith & Rainski 2004).

This book provides you with a way to make learning to read authentic and engaging for your students and yourself. Perhaps you can remember reciting poetry, singing songs, putting on plays, and giving other oral performances from your own school experience. You may not have realized that all the fun you were having was also helping to develop your reading ability! Have fun with reading. Appreciate this wonderful language of ours—a language that often needs to be practiced, performed, and heard to be fully appreciated.

Introduction

How to Use This Book

The texts in this book are engaging and enjoyable. Students will want to read, reread, and perform these texts. As they do, they will develop into fluent readers, improving their abilities to recognize words accurately and effortlessly, and read with meaningful expression and phrasing. However, you, the teacher, are the most important part in developing instruction that includes these texts.

The texts need to be read repeatedly or rehearsed over several days. Introduce one text at a time and practice it over two to five days, depending on how quickly your students develop fluent mastery. Write the text you are going to teach on chart paper or project it on an overhead transparency or in a *PowerPoint* presentation. Read the text with your students several times a day. Read it at the beginning of each day; read it during various breaks in the day; and read it at the end of each day. Encourage the students to read, rehearse, and perform their passages in a variety of ways—solos, duos, trios, quartets, whole group, choral, alternating lines, and more.

Make two copies of the text for each student. Have the students keep one copy at school in a "fluency folder." The other copy can be sent home with the students so that they can continue practicing the text with their families. Communicate to families the importance of repeated practice at school and at home.

The various sections (Poems and Rhymes, Song Lyrics, and Reader's Theater) are not presented in reading-level order. However, the pieces within each section have been sequenced from easiest to most difficult. We encourage you to stretch your students by challenging them to read passages that may seem difficult for them on initial reading. Students can often handle material that is more challenging if they have the opportunity to rehearse the passage and be guided in their rehearsal by you and other students in the class.

It is important to note, as you select texts from this book, that many traditional versions of texts have been altered and appear in various forms. The version in this book may not have the exact wording with which you are familiar. In this case, enjoy the exposure to another version of the traditional text, or feel free to type the words to the version you know, and allow your students to perform that version.

Introduction _(cont.)

Modeling Fluent Reading

Before asking your students to read a text, especially a difficult passage, read it to them and ask them to follow along silently on their copies. Ask them to listen to the way in which you use your voice to add meaning to the text. For those passages that require more than one reader, ask a fellow teacher, the school principal, an aide, a parent, or another student or students to take on the other parts of the passage.

It is critical that students develop the idea that fluency is reading with expression and meaning—not just reading fast. The most powerful way to instill this idea in students is to have them hear fluent readings by their teacher and other readers. After the readings, talk with your students about how you added to the meaning of the passage with your voice—getting louder or softer, raising and lowering your voice, reading slower and faster in various parts of the text, emphasizing words and phrases, and taking dramatic pauses.

For the fun of it, occasionally read a passage to your students disfluently— too fast, too slow, without expression, without phrasing, etc. It will not be long before students beg you to stop reading in that fashion. At that point, discuss with them what was wrong with the reading—even though you may not have made many errors, your lack of expression or fluency made for a less than satisfying reading of the text.

Coaching Your Students

Provide positive feedback as your students practice reading the target text each week: alone, in small groups, or as an entire class. Through oral interpretation of a text, readers can express joy, sadness, anger, surprise, or any variety of emotions.

Help students learn to convey emotion and meaning in their oral reading. You can do this by occasionally listening to students read and coaching them in the various aspects of oral interpretation. You may wish to suggest that students emphasize certain words, insert dramatic pauses, read a bit faster in one place, or slow down in other parts of the text. And, of course, give lavish praise for students' best efforts to convey meaning through their reading. Although it may take a while for students to develop this sense of "voice" in their readings, in the long run it will lead to more engaged and fluent readings and higher levels of comprehension.

Introduction (cont.)

Word Study

Although the aim of the fluency texts in this book is to develop fluent and meaningful oral reading of texts, practicing the passages also provides opportunities to develop students' vocabulary and word-decoding skills.

After reading a passage several times, ask the students to choose words from the passage that they think are interesting or that match a specific set of criteria you set forth, such as rhymes with *at* or *and*, sight words, or challenging but interesting words. Put these words on a word wall to which four to five new words are added daily, and ask the students to add them to their personal word banks. Talk about the meaning of each word and its spelling construction. Help the students to develop a deepened appreciation for these words, and encourage them to use them in their speech and writing. You might, for example, ask the students to use some of the chosen words in their daily journal entries. You could request that they create a silly sentence using some of the words. Most importantly, practice reading and chanting the words on the word wall several times each day.

Once a list of words has been added to your classroom word wall or students' word banks, play games with the words. A perennial favorite is Word Bingo. Give the students a card with a grid of 3 x 3, 4 x 4, or 5 x 5 boxes. In each box, the students randomly write a word from the word wall or bank. Then, you call out definitions of these words or sentences that contain the target words. The students must find the words on their cards and cover them with a marker. Once a student has covered a horizontal, vertical, or diagonal line of words, he or she calls "Bingo" and wins the game. You can then stop the game or continue play until everyone has achieved the goal.

Have the students sort the words by different parameters such as number of syllables, parts of speech, phonics features such as long vowel sound or a consonant blend, or by meaning (such as words that express how a person can feel and words that do not). Through sorting and categorizing activities, students get repeated exposure to words and analyze them in different ways.

Help students expand their vocabularies with extended word-family instruction. Choose a word from the text, like *hat*, and brainstorm with students other words that belong to the same word family (e.g., *rat, bat, scat, cattle, chatter*). Once a list of family words is chosen, have students create short poems using the rhyming words. The poems can be used for further practice and performance. No matter how you do it, make the opportunity to examine select words from these fluency passages part of your regular instructional routine. The time spent in word study will be time well spent.

Introduction (cont.)

Inflection and Expression, Not Memorization

After several days of practice, arrange a special time of day for students to perform the texts. This performance time can range from five minutes to 30 minutes, depending on the number of texts to be read. Find a special person to listen to your students perform. You may also want to invite a neighboring class, parents, school personnel, senior citizens, or another group to come to your room to listen to your students read. Have the children perform the selected text as a group. Later, you can have individuals or groups of children perform the text again.

As an alternative to having people come to your room to see the performances, you may want to send students to visit other adults and children in the building and perform for them. Principals, school secretaries, and school visitors are great audiences for children's readings. Tape-recording and videotaping your students' reading is another way to create a performance opportunity.

Regardless of how you accomplish it, it is important that you create the opportunity for your students to perform for an audience. The magic of the performance will give students more motivation to want to practice their assigned texts.

Remember, the key to developing fluency is guided-reading practice. Students become more fluent when they read the text repeatedly. Reading requires the students to actually see the words in the text. Thus, it is important that you do not require students to memorize the text they are practicing and performing. Memorization leads students away from visualizing the words. Although students may want to try to memorize some texts, your instructional emphasis needs to be on reading with expression, so that the audience will enjoy the students' oral rendering of the text. Keep students' eyes on the text as often as possible.

Introduction *(cont.)*

Reader's Theater

Reader's theater is an exciting and simple method of providing students with an opportunity to practice fluency leading up to a performance. Since reader's theater minimizes the use of props, sets, costumes, and memorization, it is an easy way to present a "play" in the classroom. Students read from scripts, using their voices to bring the texts to life. Practice for reader's theater should consist of guided repeated readings that lead to a smooth, fluent presentation.

In traditional dramas, the audience is ignored as it watches the characters perform. Reader's theater is a communication form that establishes contact with the audience. Reader's theater has the following characteristics:

- The audience has a copy of the passage so that it can follow along silently as the text is read by the performers.

- Readers use only the interpreter's tools to express emotion. These are eye contact, facial expressions, and vocal expression. The emphasis is on the vocal expressiveness.

- The script is always read; it is never memorized.

- Readers may be characters or narrators or switch back and forth into various characters and parts.

- The readers may sit, stand, or do both, but they do not have to perform any other actions.

- Scripts may be from books, songs, poems, letters, etc. They can be performed directly from the original material or adapted specifically for the reader's theater performance.

- Musical accompaniment or soundtracks may be used, but they are not necessary.

- Only simple props may be used, especially with younger children, to help the audience identify the parts.

Before assigning a reader's theater, read through all the parts. It will be apparent to you that some of the parts within a script are much easier than others. Assign the parts accordingly. If one part is especially easy, have one of your weakest readers read it to build up confidence. Another good way to support your struggling readers is to have them take a reader's theater role after it has already been performed smoothly several times by readers that are more adept.

Choral reading is an important component of learning to read fluently. Some of the reader's theater scripts call for "boys" and "girls." These parts are to be read orally by the boys as a choral group and the girls as a choral group. This supports the struggling reader by letting him or her see the text and lip-sync until feeling comfortable enough to participate.

Standards Correlations

Shell Educational Publishing is committed to producing educational materials that are research and standards-based. In this effort we have correlated all of our products to the academic standards of all 50 states, the District of Columbia, and the Department of Defense Dependent Schools. You can print a correlation report customized for your state directly from our website at **http://www.shelleducation.com.**

Purpose and Intent of Standards

The No Child Left Behind legislation mandates that all states adopt academic standards that identify the skills students will learn in kindergarten through grade twelve. While many states had already adopted academic standards prior to NCLB, the legislation set requirements to ensure the standards were detailed and comprehensive.

Standards are designed to focus instruction and guide adoption of curricula. Standards are statements that describe the criteria necessary for students to meet specific academic goals. They define the knowledge, skills, and content students should acquire at each level. Standards are also used to develop standardized tests to evaluate students' academic progress.

In many states today, teachers are required to demonstrate how their lessons meet state standards. State standards are used in development of all of our products, so educators can be assured they meet the academic requirements of each state. Complete standards correlation reports for each state can be printed directly from our website as well.

How to Find Standards Correlations

To print a correlation report for this product visit our website at **http:/www.shelleducation.com** and follow the on-screen directions. If you require assistance in printing correlation reports, please contact Customer Service at 1-877-777-3450.

Standards

The following standards are addressed as students practice and perform the texts in this book.

Language Arts
Adjusts speed of reading to suit purpose and difficulty of the material

Uses a variety of nonverbal communication skills (e.g., eye contact, gestures, facial expressions, posture)

Uses a variety of verbal communication skills (e.g., projection, tone, volume, rate, articulation, pace, phrasing)

Theater
Uses variations of locomotor and non locomotor movement and vocal pitch, tempo, and tone for different characters

Poems and Rhymes

Moses' Toeses

Moses supposes his toeses are roses,
But Moses supposes erroneously.
For nobody's toeses are posies or roses
As Moses supposes his toeses to be.

She Sells Seashells

She sells seashells by the sea shore.
The shells she sells are surely seashells.
So if she sells shells on the seashore,
I'm sure she sells seashore shells.

A Tutor

A tutor who tooted a flute
Tried to tutor two tooters to toot.
Said the two to their tutor,
"Is it harder to toot
Or to tutor two tooters to toot?"

The Odd Couple

In a cottage in Fife lived a man and his wife
Who, believe me, were comical folk.
For, to people's surprise,
They both saw with their eyes,
And their tongues moved whenever they
spoke.
When quite fast asleep,
I've been told that to keep
Their eyes open they could not contrive.
They walked on their feet,
And 'twas thought what they eat
Helped, with drinking, to keep them alive.

Stately Verse

If Mary goes far out to sea
By wayward breezed fanned,
I'd like to know—can you tell me,
Just where would Maryland?

If Tenny went high up in the air
And looked o'er land and sea,
Looked here and there and everywhere,
Say, what would Tennessee?

I looked out of the window and
Saw Orry on the lawn.
He's not there now and who can tell
Just where has Oregon?

Two girls were quarrelling one day
With garden tools, and so
I said, "My dears, let Sally rake
And just let Idaho."

An English lady had a steed.
She called him Island Bay.
She rode for exercise, and thus
Rhode Island every day.

My Kitty

by Jane Taylor

I love little kitty. Her coat is so warm.
And if I don't hurt her, she'll do me no harm.
So I'll not pull her tail, nor drive her away,
But kitty and I very gently will play.
She shall sit by my side, and I'll give her some food.
Kitty will like me because I am good.

I'll pat little kitty, and then she will purr,
And thus show her thanks for my kindness to her.
I'll not pinch her ears, nor tread on her paws,
Lest I should provoke her to use her sharp claws.
I never will vex her, nor make her displeased.
For kitty can't bear to be worried or teased.

The Silent Snake

The birds go fluttering in the air.
The rabbits run and skip.
Brown squirrels race along the bough.
The mayflies rise and dip.
But while these creatures play and leap,
The silent snake goes creepy-creep.

The birdies sing and whistle loud.
The busy insects hum.
The squirrels chat. The frogs say, "Croak,"
But the snake will always come.
Without a sound through grasses deep,
The silent snake goes creepy-creep.

A Pleasant Day

Come, my children, come away,
For the sun shines bright today.
Little children, come with me.
Birds and brooks and flowers see.
Get your hats and come away,
For it will be a pleasant day.

Everything is laughing, singing,
All the pretty flowers are springing.
See the kittens, full of fun,
Tumbling in the brilliant sun.
Children, too, may skip and play,
For it will be a pleasant day.

Bring the hoop, and bring the ball.
Come with happy faces all.
Let us make a merry ring,
Talk and laugh and dance and sing.
Quickly, quickly, come away,
For it will be a pleasant day.

Tom, Tom, the Piper's Son

Tom, Tom, the piper's son,
He learned to play when he was young.
But the only tune that he could play
Was "Over the Hills and Far Away."

Now Tom with his pipe made such a noise
That he well pleased both the girls and boys.
And they always stopped to hear him
Play "Over the Hills and Far Away."

Tom with his pipe did play with such skill
That those who heard him could ne'er keep still.
Whenever they heard him, they started to dance—
Even pigs on their hind legs would after him prance!

As Dolly was milking her cow one day,
Tom took out his pipe and began to play.
So Dolly and cow danced "The Cheshire Round"
Till the pail broke and milk spilled on the ground.

Tom met old Dame Trot with a basket of eggs.
He used his pipe, and she used her legs.
She danced about till the eggs were all broke.
She began to fret, but he laughed at the joke.

Goin' Fishing with the Wind

When the wind is in the East,
'Tis neither good for man nor beast.
When the wind is in the North,
The skillful fisher goes not forth.
When the wind is in the South,
It blows the bait from the fish's mouth.
When the wind is in the West,
Then 'tis at the very best.

The Man Who Had Naught

There was a poor man and he had naught,
And thieves they came to rob him.
He crept right up the chimney pot,
And then they thought they had him.
But he went down the other side,
And then they could not find him.
He ran 14 miles in 15 days
And never looked behind him!

Mrs. Mason's Basin

Mrs. Mason bought a basin.
Mrs. Tyson said, "What a nice 'un."
"What did it cost?" said Mrs. Frost.
"Half a crown," said Mrs. Brown.
"Did it indeed?" said Mrs. Reed.
"It did for certain," said Mrs. Burton.
Then Mrs. Nix got up to her tricks,
And threw the basin on the bricks!

Hurt No Living Thing

by Christina Rossetti

Hurt no living thing,
Ladybird, nor butterfly,
Nor moth with dusty wing,
Nor cricket chirping cheerily,
Nor grasshopper so light of leap,
Nor dancing gnat, nor beetle fat,
Nor harmless worms that creep.

Simple Simon

Simple Simon met a pieman going to the fair.
Said Simple Simon to the pieman, "Let me taste your ware."

Said the pieman to Simple Simon, "Show me first your penny."
Said Simple Simon to the pieman, "Indeed, I have not any."

Then Simple Simon went a-fishing for to catch a whale;
But all the water he had got was in his mother's pail.
He went to shoot a wild duck, but the plump duck flew away.
Said Simon, "I can't hit him, because he will not stay!"

Simple Simon went to look if plums grew on a thistle.
He pricked his finger very much, which made poor Simon whistle.
He went to slide upon the ice before the ice could bear.
Then he plunged in above his knees, which made poor Simon glare.

Simple Simon went for water with a sieve, and soon it all ran through.
So now, poor Simple Simon bids you all adieu.

Grasshopper Green

Grasshopper Green is a comical chap.
He lives on the best of fare.
Bright little trousers, jacket, and cap;
These are his summer wear.
Out in the meadow he loves to go,
Playing away in the sun.
It's hopperty, skipperty, high and low—
Summer's the time for fun!

Grasshopper Green has a quaint little house.
It's under the hedge so gay.
Grandmother Spider, as still as a mouse,
Watches him over the way.
Gladly he's calling the children, I know,
Out in the beautiful sun.
It's hopperty, skipperty, high and low—
Summer's the time for fun!

The Eagle

by Lord Alfred Tennyson

He clasps the crag with crooked hands;
Close to the sun in lonely lands,
Ringed with azure world, he stands.

The wrinkled sea beneath him crawls;
He watches from his mountain walls,
And like a thunderbolt he falls.

Give Me the Splendid Silent Sun

by Walt Whitman

Give me the splendid silent sun with all its beams full-dazzling.
Give me juicy autumnal fruit, ripe and red from the orchard.
Give me a field where unmowed grass grows.
Give me an arbor, give me the trellised grape.
Give me fresh corn and wheat, give me serene-moving
    animals, teaching content.

The Land of Story-Books

by Robert Louis Stevenson

In evening when the lamp is lit,
Around the fire my parents sit;
They sit at home and talk and sing,
And do not play at anything.

Now with my little gun I crawl
All in the dark along the wall,
And follow 'round the forest track
Away behind the sofa back.

There, in the night, where none can spy,
All in my hunter's camp I lie,
And play at books that I have read
Till it is time to go to bed.

These are the hills, these are the woods,
These are my starry solitudes;
And there the river by whose brink
The roaring lions come to drink.

The Land of Story-Books (cont.)

I see the others far away
As if in firelit camp they lay,
And I, like to an Indian scout,
Around their party prowled about.

So when my nurse comes in for me,
Home I return across the sea,
And go to bed with backward looks
At my dear Land of Story-Books.

Allergies

by Debra Jean Housel

The doctor says I have allergies,
And that's why some things make me sneeze.
So I have to be careful about what I do,
Or I get symptoms like the flu.

My nose starts to twitch and my eyes will itch
If I stop to pick flowers alongside a ditch.
And if I don't want to break out in red hives,
I can only pet stuffed cats and not those alive.

Every spring it's the same old story—
The grass and the trees come out in their glory.
So every year it's no big surprise
That my eyes look like I've cried and cried.

Sometimes kids tease when I sniffle and wheeze
Because of my dreadful allergies.
But they will find out if they live long enough
That they are allergic to some sort of stuff!

To Every Thing There Is a Season

Ecclesiastes from the King James Bible

To every thing there is a season,
And a time to every purpose under heaven.
A time to be born, and a time to die;
A time to plant, and a time to pluck up that which is planted;
A time to kill, and a time to heal;
A time to break down, and a time to build up;
A time to weep, and a time to laugh;
A time to mourn, and a time to dance;
A time to cast away stones, and a time to gather stones together;
A time to embrace, and a time to refrain from embracing;
A time to seek, and a time to lose;
A time to keep, and a time to cast away;
A time to rend, and a time to sew;
A time to keep silent, and a time to speak;
A time to love, and a time to hate;
A time for war, and a time for peace.

The Grass

by Emily Dickinson

The grass has so little to do—a sphere of simple green,
With only butterflies to brood and bees to entertain.
And stir all day to pretty tunes the breezes fetch along,
And hold the sunshine in its lap and bow to everything.
And thread the dews all night like pearls and make itself so fine
A duchess were too common for such a noticing.
And even when it dies to pass in odors so divine,
As lowly spices gone to sleep on amulets of pine.
And then to dwell in sovereign barns and dream the days away—
The grass so little has to do: I wish I were the hay!

Song of the Sky Loom

Traditional Pueblo song

O, our Mother the Earth! O, our Father the Sky!
Your children are we.
And with tired backs we bring you the gifts that you love.
Then weave for us a garment of brightness.
May the warp be the white light of morning.
May the weft be the red light of evening.
May the fringes be the falling rain.
May the border be the standing rainbow.
Thus weave for us a garment of brightness
That we may walk fittingly where birds sing,
That we may walk fittingly where grass is green.
O, our Mother the Earth! O, our Father the Sky!

The Daffodils

by William Wordsworth

I wandered lonely as a cloud
That floats on high o'er vales and hills,
When all at once I saw a crowd,
A host, of golden daffodils;
Beside the lake, beneath the trees,
Fluttering and dancing in the breeze.

Continuous as the stars that shine
And twinkle in the Milky Way.
They stretched in never-ending line
Along the margin of a bay:
Ten thousand saw I at a glance,
Tossing their heads in sprightly dance.

The waves beside them dance, but they
Outdid the sparkling waves in glee.
A poet could not be but gay
In such a jovial company.
I gazed—and gazed—but little thought
What wealth the show to me had brought.

For oft, when on my couch I lie
In vacant or in pensive mood,
They flash upon that inward eye
Which is the bliss of solitude.
And then my heart with pleasure fills,
And dances with the daffodils.

The Story of Fidgety Philip

by Dr. Heinrich Hoffman

Let us see if Philip can
Be a little gentleman.
Let us see if he is able
To sit still for once at the table.

But Philip, he did not mind
His parents who were so kind.
He wriggled
And giggled,
And then, I declare,
Swung backward and forward
And tilted his chair.

See the naughty, restless child,
Growing still more rude and wild,
Till his chair crashes on the floor.
Philip screams with a mighty roar,
Catches at the cloth, but then
That makes matters worse again.
Down upon the ground they fall,
Glasses, bread, forks and all.

How Mamma did fret and frown,
When she saw them tumbling down!
And Papa made such a face!
Philip is in sad disgrace.

On the Bridge

by Kate Greenaway

If I could see a little fish—
That is what I just now wish!
I want to see his great round eyes
Always open in surprise.

I wish a water-rat would glide
Slowly to the other side,
Or a dancing spider sit
On the yellow flags a bit.

I think I'll get some stones to throw,
And watch the pretty circles show.
Or shall we sail a flower boat,
And watch it slowly—slowly float?

That's nice—because you never know
How far away it means to go.
And when tomorrow comes, you see,
It may be in the great wide sea.

New Year Snow

by Edith Nesbit

The white snow falls on hill and dale,
The snow falls white by square and street,
Falls on the town, a bridal veil,
And on the fields a winding-sheet.

A winding-sheet for last year's flowers,
For last year's love, and last year's tear,
A bridal veil for the New Hours,
For the New Love and the New Year.

Soft snow, spread out his winding-sheet!
Spin fine her veil, O bridal snow!
Cover the print of her dancing feet,
And the place where he lies low.

Ice Town

by Katrina Eileen Housel

What if the town were made all of ice?
The buildings all shiny, slippery, and nice.
The streets filled with music, sound bouncing around,
While kids in ice skates spun on the ground.

We'd wear visors to save us from the bright glare.
There'd be no cars, just cold, clean, crisp air.
A chilly place to cuddle close—freezing, but fun,
Till the town melts away in the warm springtime sun.

A Serenade for New Year's Eve

The old year departed, how swiftly it flew.
'Tis gone and with rapture we welcome the new.
We trust a bright morning will dawn on your eyes,
And sun beams unclouded illumine the skies.
Then wake from your slumbers, our serenade hear.
We wish you a happy, a happy New Year!

Song for a Little House

by Christopher Morley

I'm glad our house is a little house,
Not too tall nor too wide.
I'm glad the hovering butterflies
Feel free to come inside.

Our little house is a friendly house.
It is not shy or vain;
It gossips with the talking trees,
And makes friends with the rain.

And quick leaves cast a shimmer of green
Against our whited walls.
And in the phlox, the dutious bees
Are paying duty calls.

O Wind, Why Do You Never Rest?

by Christina Rossetti

O wind, why do you never rest
Wandering, whistling to and fro,
Bringing rain out of the west,
From the dim north bringing snow?

The Vulture

by Hillaire Belloc

The vulture eats between his meals,
And that's the reason why
He very, very, rarely feels
As well as you and I.

His eye is dull. His head is bald.
His neck is growing thinner.
Oh! What a lesson for us all
To only eat at dinner!

Little Raindrops

by Jane Euphemia Browne

Oh, where do you come from,
You little drops of rain,
Pitter patter, pitter patter,
Down the window pane?

They won't let me walk,
And they won't let me play,
And they won't let me go
Out of doors at all today.

They put away my playthings
Because I broke them all,
And then they locked up all my bricks,
And took away my ball.

Tell me, little raindrops,
Is that the way you play,
Pitter patter, pitter patter,
All the rainy day?

Little Raindrops (cont.)

They say I'm very naughty,
But I've nothing else to do
But sit here at the window.
I should like to play with you.
The little raindrops cannot speak,
But "pitter pitter pat"
Means, "We can play on this side,
Why can't you play on that?"

Wishing

by Ella Wheeler Wilcox

Do you wish the world were better?
Let me tell you what to do.
Set a watch upon your actions,
Keep them always straight and true.
Rid your mind of selfish motives,
Let your thoughts be clean and high.
You can make a little Eden
Of the sphere you occupy.

Do you wish the world were wiser?
Well, suppose you make a start,
By accumulating wisdom
In the scrapbook of your heart;
Do not waste one page on folly;
Live to learn, and learn to live
If you want to give men knowledge
You must get it, ere you give.

Do you wish the world were happy?
Then remember day by day
Just to scatter seeds of kindness
As you pass along the way,
For the pleasures of many
May be ofttimes traced to one,
As the hand that plants an acorn
Shelters armies from the sun.

The Window

by Walter de la Mare

Behind the blinds I sit and watch
The people passing—passing by.
And not a single one can see
My tiny watching eye.

They cannot see my little room,
All yellowed with the shaded sun.
They do not even know I'm here.
Nor'll guess when I am gone.

What Do the Stars Do?

by Christina Rossetti

What do the stars do
Up in the sky,
Higher than the wind can blow,
Or the clouds can fly?
Each star in its own glory
Circles, circles still,
As it was lit to shine and set,
And do its Maker's will.

The Cat of Cats

by William Brighty Rands

I am the cat of cats. I am
The everlasting cat!
Cunning, and old, and sleek as jam.
The everlasting cat!
I hunt vermin in the night—
The everlasting cat!
For I see best without the light—
The everlasting cat!

Eletelephony

by Laura E. Richards

Once there was an elephant,
Who tried to use the telephant...
No! No! I mean an elephone...
Who tried to use the telephone...
(Dear me! I am not certain quite
That even now I've got it right.)

Howe'er it was, he got his trunk
Entangled in the telephunk.
The more he tried to get it free,
The louder buzzed the telephee...
(I fear I'd better drop the song
Of elephop and telephong!)

  #50443 *Building Fluency Through Practice and Performance—Grade 3*

Tit for Tat

by Christopher Morley

I often pass a gracious tree
Whose name I can't identify,
But still I bow, in courtesy.
It waves a bough, in kind reply.

I do not know your name, O tree.
Are you a hemlock or a pine?
But why should that embarrass me?
Quite probably you don't know mine.

Song Lyrics

Song Lyrics

When Johnny Comes Marching Home Again

by Patrick S. Gilmore

When Johnny comes marching home again,
Hurrah! Hurrah!
We'll give him a hearty welcome then,
Hurrah! Hurrah!
The men will cheer and the boys will shout.
And the ladies they will all turn out,
And we'll all say, "Yay,"
When Johnny comes marching home.

The old church bell will peal with joy,
Hurrah! Hurrah!
To welcome home our darling boy,
Hurrah! Hurrah!
The village lads and lassies say
With roses they will strew the way,
And we'll all say, "Hey,"
When Johnny comes marching home.

Get ready for the Jubilee,
Hurrah! Hurrah!
We'll give the hero three times three,
Hurrah! Hurrah!
The laurel wreath is ready now
To place upon his loyal brow,
And we'll all say, "Yay,"
When Johnny comes marching home.

When Johnny Comes Marching Home Again *(cont.)*

When Johnny comes marching home again,
Hurrah! Hurrah!
We'll give him a hearty welcome then,
Hurrah! Hurrah!
The men will cheer and the boys will shout
And the ladies they will all turn out,
And we'll all say, "Yay,"
When Johnny comes marching home.

Look for the Silver Lining

by Buddy DeSylva

Please don't be offended if I preach to you awhile.
Tears are out of place in eyes that were meant to smile.
There's a way to make your very biggest troubles small.
Here's the happy secret of it all.

Look for the silver lining
When e'er a cloud appears in the blue.
Remember somewhere the sun is shining,
And so the right thing to do
Is make it shine for you.

A heart, full of joy and gladness
Will always banish sadness and strife.
So always look for the silver lining,
And try to find the sunny side of life.

Look for the silver lining
When e'er a cloud appears in the blue.
Remember somewhere the sun is shining,
And so the right thing to do
Is make it shine for you.

A heart, full of joy and gladness
Will always banish sadness and strife.
So always look for the silver lining,
And try to find the sunny side of life.

My Grandfather's Clock

My grandfather's clock
Was too large for the shelf,
So it stood ninety years on the floor.
It was taller by half
Than the old man himself,
Though it weighed not a pennyweight more.
It was bought on the morn'
Of the day that he was born
And was always his treasure and pride.

But it stopped short
Never to go again
When the old man died.
Ninety years without slumbering,
Tick, tock, tick, tock.
His life seconds numbering,
Tick, tock, tick, tock.
It stopped short
Never to go again
When the old man died.

My Grandfather's Clock (cont.)

My grandfather said
That of those he could hire,
Not a servant so faithful he found.
For it wasted no time
And had but one desire
At the close of each week to be wound.
And it kept in its place,
Not a frown upon its face,
And its hand never hung by its side.

But it stopped short
Never to go again
When the old man died.
Ninety years without slumbering,
Tick, tock, tick, tock.
His life seconds numbering,
Tick, tock, tick, tock.
It stopped short
Never to go again
When the old man died.

My Grandfather's Clock (cont.)

In watching its pendulum
Swing to and fro,
Many hours had he spent while a boy.
And in childhood and manhood
The clock seemed to know
And to share both his grief and his joy.
For it struck twenty-four
When he entered at the door.
With a blooming and beautiful bride.

But it stopped short
Never to go again
When the old man died.
Ninety years without slumbering,
Tick, tock, tick, tock.
His life seconds numbering,
Tick, tock, tick, tock.
It stopped short
Never to go again
When the old man died.

My Grandfather's Clock *(cont.)*

It rang an alarm
In the dead of the night,
An alarm that for years had been dumb.
And we knew that his spirit
Was pluming for flight,
That his hour of departure had come.
Still the clock kept the time
With its soft and muffled chime
As we proudly stood by his side.

But it stopped short
Never to go again
When the old man died.
Ninety years without slumbering,
Tick, tock, tick, tock.
His life seconds numbering,
Tick, tock, tick, tock.
It stopped short
Never to go again,
When the old man died.

It stopped short
Never to go again,
When the old man died.

Down in the Valley

Down in the valley, valley so low,
Hang your head over, hear the wind blow.
Hear the wind blow, love, hear the wind blow.
Hang your head over, hear the wind blow.

Roses love sunshine. Violets love dew.
Angels in heaven know I love you.
Know I love you, love, know I love you,
Angels in heaven know I love you.

Down in the valley, valley so low,
Hang your head over, hear the wind blow.
Hear the wind blow, love, hear the wind blow.
Hang your head over, hear the wind blow.

If you don't love me, love whom you please.
Throw your arms 'round me, give my heart ease.
Give my heart ease, love, give my heart ease,
Throw your arms 'round me, give my heart ease.

Down in the valley, valley so low,
Hang your head over, hear the wind blow.
Hear the wind blow, love, hear the wind blow.
Hang your head over, hear the wind blow.

Down in the Valley *(cont.)*

Build me a castle, forty feet high,
So I can see her as she rides by.
As she rides by, love, as she rides by,
So I can see her as she rides by.

Down in the valley, valley so low,
Hang your head over, hear the wind blow.
Hear the wind blow, love, hear the wind blow.
Hang your head over, hear the wind blow.

Write me a letter. And send it by mail.
Send it in care of the Birmingham jail.
Birmingham jail, love, Birmingham jail,
Send it in care of the Birmingham jail.

Down in the valley, valley so low,
Hang your head over, hear the wind blow.
Hear the wind blow, love, hear the wind blow.
Hang your head over, hear the wind blow.

Li'l Liza Jane

I know a gal that I adore, Li'l Li-za Jane.
Way down south in Baltimore, Li'l Li-za Jane.

Oh, Li'l Li-za, Li'l Li-za Jane.
Oh, Li'l Li-za, Li'l Li-za Jane.

I don't care how far we roam, Li'l Li-za Jane.
Where you are at will be my home, Li'l Li-za Jane.

Oh, Li'l Li-za, Li'l Li-za Jane.
Oh, Li'l Li-za, Li'l Li-za Jane.

You got a gal and I got none, Li'l Li-za Jane.
Come my love and be my one, Li'l Li-za Jane.

Oh, Li'l Li-za, Li'l Li-za Jane.
Oh, Li'l Li-za, Li'l Li-za Jane.

Liza Jane looks good to me, Li'l Li-za Jane.
Sweetest gal I ever did see, Li'l Li-za Jane.

Oh, Li'l Li-za, Li'l Li-za Jane.
Oh, Li'l Li-za, Li'l Li-za Jane.

I got a house in Baltimore, Li'l Li-za Jane.
Posies growing 'round the door, Li'l Li-za Jane.

Oh, Li'l Li-za, Li'l Li-za Jane.
Oh, Li'l Li-za, Li'l Li-za Jane.

Come my love and marry me, Li'l Li-za Jane.
I will take good care of thee, Li'l Li-za Jane.

Oh, Li'l Li-za, Li'l Li-za Jane.
Oh, Li'l Li-za, Li'l Li-za Jane.

Oh, Li'l Li-za.
Oh, Li'l Li-za.

My Old Kentucky Home

The sun shines bright on my old Kentucky home.
'Tis summer, the trees are in sway.
The corn top's ripe and the meadow's in bloom
While the birds make music all the day.
The young folks roll on the little cabin floor,
All merry, all happy, and bright.
By 'n by hard times come a-knocking at the door,
Then my old Kentucky home, good night.

Weep no more, my lady.
Oh, weep no more, today.
We will sing one song for the old Kentucky home,
For the old Kentucky home far away.

They hunt no more for the 'possum and the coon
On meadow, the hill and the shore.
They sing no more by the glimmer of the moon
On the bench by that old cabin door.
The day goes by like a shadow o'er the heart
With sorrow where all was delight.
The time has come when the workers have to part
Then my old Kentucky home, good night.

My Old Kentucky Home (cont.)

Weep no more, my lady.
Oh, weep no more, today.
We will sing one song for the old Kentucky home,
For the old Kentucky home far away.

The head must bow and the back will have to bend,
Wherever the poor folks may go.
A few more days and the trouble will end.
In the field where sugar canes may grow.
A few more days for to tote the weary load.
No matter, 'twill never be light.
A few more days till we totter on the road,
Then my old Kentucky home, good night.

Weep no more, my lady.
Oh, weep no more, today.
We will sing one song for the old Kentucky home,
For the old Kentucky home far away.

Old Dan Tucker

Went to town the other night
To hear a noise and see a fight.
All the folks was running around,
Said Old Dan Tucker's a-coming to town.

Get out of the way for Old Dan Tucker.
It's too late to get his supper.
Supper's over and dinner's cookin'.
Old Dan Tucker just standin' there lookin'.

Well, Old Dan Tucker he come to town.
Ridin' a billy goat, leadin' a hound.
Well, the hound dog barked and the billy goat jumped.
They throwed Dan Tucker and he straddled a stump.

Get out of the way for Old Dan Tucker.
It's too late to get his supper.
Supper's over and dinner's cookin'.
Old Dan Tucker just standin' there lookin'.

Old Dan Tucker *(cont.)*

Old Dan Tucker was a fine old man.
Washed his face in a frying pan.
He combed his hair with a wagon wheel,
And died with a toothache in his heel.

Get out of the way for Old Dan Tucker.
It's too late to get his supper.
Supper's over and dinner's cookin'.
Old Dan Tucker just standin' there lookin'.

Get out of the way for Old Dan Tucker.
It's too late to get his supper.
Supper's over and dinner's cookin'.
Old Dan Tucker just standin' there lookin'.

Hey, Ho, Nobody Home

Sung as a round

Hey, ho, nobody home.
Meat nor drink nor money have I none.
Yet will I be merry.

Simple Gifts

'Tis the gift to be simple.
'Tis the gift to be free.
'Tis the gift to come down
Where we ought to be.

And when we find ourselves
In the place just right,
It will be in the valley
Of love and delight.

When true
Simplicity is gained,
To bow and to bend,
We will not be ashamed.

To turn, turn,
Will be our delight,
'Til by turning, turning,
We come 'round right.

Swing Low, Sweet Chariot

Swing low, sweet chariot,
Coming for to carry me home.
Swing low, sweet chariot,
Coming for to carry me home.

I looked over Jordan, and what
    did I see,
Coming for to carry me home?
A band of angels coming
    after me,
Coming for to carry me home.

Swing low, sweet chariot,
Coming for to carry me home.
Swing low, sweet chariot,
Coming for to carry me home.

If you get there before I do,
Coming for to carry me home,
Tell all my friends I'm coming too,
Coming for to carry me home.

Swing low, sweet chariot,
Coming for to carry me home.
Swing low, sweet chariot,
Coming for to carry me home.

I'm sometimes up, I'm
    sometimes down,
Coming for to carry me home,
But still my soul feels
    heavenly bound,
Coming for to carry me home.

Swing low, sweet chariot,
Coming for to carry me home.
Swing low, sweet chariot,
Coming for to carry me home.

This Little Light of Mine

This little light of mine,
I'm going to let it shine.
This little light of mine,
I'm going to let it shine.
This little light of mine,
I'm going to let it shine,
Let it shine, let it shine, let it shine.

Ev'ry where I go
I'm going to let it shine.
Oh, ev'ry where I go
I'm going to let it shine, Hallelujah
Ev'ry where I go
I'm going to let it shine
Let it shine, let it shine, let it shine.

All in my house
I'm going to let it shine
Oh, all in my house
I'm going to let it shine
All in my house
I'm going to let it shine
Let it shine, let it shine, let it shine.

This Little Light of Mine *(cont.)*

I'm not going to make it shine,
I'm just going to let it shine.
I'm not going to make it shine,
I'm just going to let it shine.
I'm not going to make it shine,
I'm just going to let it shine.
Let it shine, let it shine, let it shine.

Out in the dark
I'm going to let it shine.
Oh, out in the dark
I'm going to let it shine.
Out in the dark
I'm going to let it shine.
Let it shine, let it shine, let it shine.

This little light of mine,
I'm going to let it shine.
This little light of mine,
I'm going to let it shine.
This little light of mine,
I'm going to let it shine,
Let it shine, let it shine, let it shine.

Alberta

Alberta, let your hair hang low.
Alberta, let your hair hang low.
I'll give you more gold than your apron can hold
If you'll just let your hair hang low.

Alberta, what's on your mind?
Alberta, what's on your mind?
You keep me worried, you keep me bothered all the time.
Alberta, what's on your mind?

Alberta, don't treat me unkind.
Alberta, don't treat me unkind.
My heart feels sad 'cause I want you so bad.
Alberta, don't treat me unkind.

Alberta, let your hair hang low.
Alberta, let your hair hang low.
I'll give you more gold than your apron can hold
If you'll just let your hair hang low.

Cindy

You ought to see my Cindy.
She lives away down south.
She's so sweet the honeybees
All swarm around her mouth.

Get along home, Cindy, Cindy.
Get along home.
Get along home, Cindy, Cindy.
I'll marry you some day.

Wish I was an apple
A-hangin' on a tree,
An' every time that Cindy passed,
She'd take a bite o' me.

Get along home, Cindy, Cindy.
Get along home.
Get along home, Cindy, Cindy.
I'll marry you some day.

She took me to the parlor.
She cooled me with her fan.
She said I was the prettiest thing
In the shape of mortal man.

Cindy (cont.)

Get along home, Cindy, Cindy.
Get along home.
Get along home, Cindy, Cindy.
I'll marry you some day.

Cindy in the summertime,
Cindy in the fall.
If I can't have Cindy all the time,
Have no one at all.

Get along home, Cindy, Cindy.
Get along home.
Get along home, Cindy, Cindy.
I'll marry you some day.

If I had a pretty gal,
I'd put her on a shelf.
Ev'ry time she smiled at me,
I'd jump right up myself.

Get along home, Cindy, Cindy.
Get along home.
Get along home, Cindy, Cindy.
I'll marry you some day.

Cindy *(cont.)*

Cindy had one blue eye.
She also had one brown.
One eye looked in the country.
The other one in the town.

Get along home, Cindy, Cindy.
Get along home.
Get along home, Cindy, Cindy.
I'll marry you some day.

Wish I had a needle and thread,
Wish that I could sew.
I'd sew that gal to my coattails
And down the road we'd go.

Reader's Theater Scripts

The Flag Goes By

by Henry Holcomb Bennett
A reader's theater script for four voices

All: Hats off!

Reader 1:   Along the street there comes a blare of bugles,

Reader 2:   A ruffle of drums,

Reader 3:   A flash of color beneath the sky:

All: Hats off!

Reader 4:   The flag is passing by!

Reader 1:   Blue and crimson and white it shines,

Reader 2:   Over the steel-tipped, ordered lines.

All: Hats off!

Reader 3:   The colors before us fly;

Reader 4:   But more than the flag is passing by.

Reader 1:   Sea-fights and land-fights, grim and great,

Reader 2:   Fought to make and to save the State:

Reader 3:   Weary marches and sinking ships;

Reader 4:   Cheers of victory on dying lips;

The Flag Goes By *(cont.)*

Reader 1:   Days of plenty and years of peace;

Reader 2:   March of a strong land's swift increase;

Reader 3:   Equal justice, right and law,

Reader 4:   Stately honor and reverend awe;

Reader 1:   Sign of a nation, great and strong to ward her people from foreign wrong:

Reader 2:   Pride and glory and honor—

Reader 3:   All live in the colors to stand or fall.

All: Hats off!

Reader 1:   Along the street there comes a blare of bugles,

Reader 2:   A ruffle of drums;

Reader 3:   And loyal hearts are beating high:

Reader 4:   Hats off!

All: The flag is passing by!

The Easter Bunny

by M. Josephine Todd
A reader's theater script for four voices

Reader 1:   There's a story quite funny,
                  about a toy bunny,

Reader 2:   And the wonderful things she can do;

Reader 3:   Every bright Easter morning,

Reader 4:   Without warning,

All: She colors eggs, red, green, or blue.

Reader 1:   Some she covers with spots,

Reader 2:   Some with quaint little dots,

Readers 1 & 2: And some with strange mixed colors, too.

Reader 3:   Red and green, blue and yellow,

Reader 4:   But each unlike his fellow

The Easter Bunny *(cont.)*

Readers 3 & 4: Are eggs of every hue.

Reader 1: And it's odd, as folks say,
That on no other day

Reader 2: In all of the whole year through,

Reader 3: Does this wonderful bunny,

Reader 4: So busy and funny,

All: Color eggs of every hue.

Reader 1: If this story you doubt

Reader 2: She will soon find you out,

Reader 3: And what do you think she will do?

Reader 4: On the next Easter morning,

All: She'll bring you without warning,
Those eggs of every hue.

A Modern Occupational Alphabet

A reader's theater for 13 voices

Reader 1:   A was an artist who painted with oils.

Reader 2:   B was a banker who all day would toil.

All: An artist, a banker who all day would toil.

Reader 3:   C was a chemist who worked with chlorine.

Reader 4:   D was a dentist who checked for hygiene.

All: A chemist, a dentist who checked for hygiene.

Reader 5:   E was an engineer who designed huge towers.

Reader 6:   F was a florist who arranged exotic flowers.

All: An engineer, a florist who arranged
exotic flowers.

Reader 7:   G was a geologist who excavated rocks.

Reader 8:   H was a housekeeper who paired up the socks.

A Modern Occupational Alphabet (cont.)

All: A geologist, a housekeeper who paired up the socks.

Reader 9:   I was an illustrator whose paints he would lose.

Reader 10: J was a journalist who wrote up the news.

All: An illustrator, a journalist who wrote up the news.

Reader 11: K was a kindergarten teacher who taught the fives.

Reader 12: L was a lifeguard who liked to save lives.

All: A kindergarten teacher, a lifeguard who liked to save lives.

Reader 13: M was a mail clerk who sorted by zip code.

Reader 1:   N was a nurse with a huge patient load.

All: A mail clerk, a nurse with a huge patient load.

Reader 2:   O was an operator who connected the numbers.

Reader 3:   P was a pharmacist who helped people slumber.

A Modern Occupational Alphabet (cont.)

All: An operator, a pharmacist who helped people slumber.

Reader 4: Q was a quality controller who checked on the spam.

Reader 5: R was a researcher who studied Amsterdam.

All: A quality controller, a researcher who studied Amsterdam.

Reader 6: S was a scientist who studied the crickets.

Reader 7: T was a travel agent who found us great tickets.

All: A scientist, a travel agent who found us great tickets.

Reader 8: U was an urban planner who restored neighborhoods.

Reader 9: V was a veterinarian who did critters good.

All: An urban planner, a veterinarian who did critters good.

A Modern Occupational Alphabet (cont.)

Reader 10: W was a Web designer who created Web pages.

Reader 11: X was an X-ray technician who could see our rib cages.

All: A Web designer, an X-ray technician who could see our rib cages.

Reader 12: Y was a yoga instructor who would stretch and extend.

Reader 13: Z was a zookeeper, with animals to tend.

All: A yoga instructor, a zookeeper with animals to tend.

Performance Note: When performing this reader's theater script, you might want the readers to carry alphabet letters on reversible large cards. For example, the first reader's card would have an A on one side with an N on the other. To incorporate technology, the children can create *PowerPoint* slides for each of their letters and vocations.

Friendly Beasts

*A reader's theater script for six voices: two narrators,
a donkey, a cow, a sheep, and a dove*

Narrator 1: Jesus our brother,

Narrator 2: Strong and good,

Narrator 1: Was humbly born in a stable of wood,

Narrator 2: And the friendly beasts around Him stood,

Animals: Jesus our brother, strong and good.

Donkey: "I,"

Narrator 1: Said the donkey, shaggy and brown,

Donkey: "I carried His mother up hill and down,
I carried her safely to Bethlehem town; I,"

Narrator 1: Said the donkey, shaggy and brown.

Cow: "I,"

Narrator 2: Said the cow, all white and red,

Cow: "I gave Him my manger for His bed,
I gave Him my hay to pillow His head; I,"

Narrator 2: Said the cow, all white and red.

Friendly Beasts <small>(cont.)</small>

Sheep: "I,"

Narrator 1: Said the sheep, with curly horn,

Sheep: "I gave Him my wool for His blanket torn,
He wore my coat on Christmas morn; I,"

Narrator 1: Said the sheep, with curly horn.

Dove: "I,"

Narrator 2: Said the dove, from the rafters high,

Dove: "Cooed Him to sleep, my mate and I,
We cooed Him to sleep, my mate and I; I,"

Narrator 2: Said the dove, from the rafters high.

Narrator 1: And every beast,

Narrator 2: By some good spell,

Narrator 1: In the stable dark was glad to tell,

Narrator 2: Of the gift he gave Immanuel,

Animals: The gifts we gave Immanuel.

The Funniest Thing in the World

by James Whitcomb Riley
A rhythmic reader's theater for many voices: two groups of students

Group 1: The funniest thing in the world, I know,
Is watchin' the monkeys' 'at's in the show!

Group 2: Jumpin' an' runnin' an' racin' roun',
Way up the top o' the pole; nen down!

Group 1: First they're here,

Group 2: an' nen they're there,

All: An' ist a'most any an' ever'where!

Group 1: Screechin' an' scratchin' wherever they go,

Group 2: They're the funniest thing in the world, I know!

Group 1: They're the funniest thing in the world, I think:
Funny to watch 'em eat an' drink;

Group 2: Funny to watch 'em a-watchin' us,
An' actin' 'most like grown folks does!

Group 1: Funny to watch 'em p'tend to be
Skeerd at their tail 'at they happen to see;

Group 2: But the funniest thing in the world they do

All: Is never to laugh, like me an' you!

Performance Note: James Whitcomb Riley wrote poetry in a Midwestern dialect. After you have learned how to pronounce all of the words in spite of the missing letter sounds, begin to work on the rhythm of this piece. You can actually play some rhythm instruments along with the oral reading to add to the piece's effect.

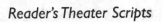

How the Leaves Came Down

Poem by Susan Coolidge
A reader's theater script for eight voices: a tree, four readers, and three leaves

Tree: "I'll tell you how the leaves came down,"

Reader 1: The great tree to his children said,

Tree: "You're getting sleepy, Yellow and Brown,
Yes, very sleepy, little Red.
It is quite time to go to bed."

Leaves: "Ah!"

Reader 2: Begged each silly, pouting leaf,

Leaf 1: "Let us a little longer stay;

Leaf 2: Dear Father Tree, behold our grief;

Leaf 3: Tis such a very pleasant day

Leaf 1: We do not want to go away."

Reader 3: So, for just one more merry day
To the great tree the leaflets clung,

Reader 1: Frolicked and danced, and had their way,
Upon the autumn breezes swung,
Whispering all their sports among,—

Leaf 1: "Perhaps the great tree will forget,

Leaf 2: And let us stay until the spring,

Leaf 3: If we all beg, and coax, and fret."

Reader 3: But the great tree did no such thing;

How the Leaves Came Down *(cont.)*

Reader 4:   He smiled to hear their whispering.

Tree: "Come, children, all to bed,"

Reader 2:   He cried;

Reader 3:   And ere the leaves could urge their prayer,
He shook his head,

Reader 4:   And far and wide,
Fluttering and rustling everywhere,
Down sped the leaflets through the air.

Reader 1:   I saw them; on the ground they lay,

Reader 2:   Golden and red, a huddled swarm,

Reader 3:   Waiting till one from far away,
White bedclothes heaped upon her arm,

Reader 4:   Should come to wrap them safe and warm.

Reader 1:   The great bare tree looked down and smiled,

Tree: "Good-night, dear little leaves,"

Reader 2:   He said.

Reader 3:   And from below each sleepy child replied,

Leaves: "Good-night,"

Reader 4:   And murmured,

Leaves: "It is so nice to go to bed!"

Butterflies and Moths

A reader's theater for six butterflies and six moths

All Butterflies:	We are the butterflies.
All Moths:	We are the moths.
Butterfly 1 & Moth 1:	Some people can't tell us apart!
Butterfly 2 & Moth 2:	But we are very different!
Butterfly 3 & Moth 3:	We all belong to the same group of insects.
Butterfly 4 & Moth 4:	We all have six legs.
Butterfly 5 & Moth 5:	We all have scales on our wings. They feel like powder when they are touched.
All:	We are called Lepidoptera (Leh-pih-DOP-ter-ra), meaning "scaly winged."
Butterfly 6 & Moth 6:	We all spread pollen from flower to flower.
Butterfly 1:	But I love to fly around in the bright hot sunshine.
Moth 1:	And I love to flutter around the glow of streetlights at night.
Butterfly 2:	My colors and patterns are as brilliant as the flowers I love to fly around.
Moth 2:	My soft coloring and quiet patterns allow me to rest against the bark of a tree all day long.

 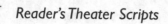

Butterflies and Moths (cont.)

Butterfly 3: I rest with my wings up.

Moth 3: I rest with my wings out.

Butterfly 4 & Moth 4: We have an exoskeleton that is divided into three sections: the head, thorax, and abdomen.

Butterfly 4: But I have a slender, hairless body.

Moth 4: And I have a fat abdomen and furry body.

Butterfly 5 & Moth 5: We have antennae. We use them to taste, feel, and smell.

Butterfly 5: But my antennae have clubs or hooks on the tips.

Moth 5: And my antennae are feathery, and thicker than a butterfly's.

Butterfly 6 & Moth 6: We both go through metamorphosis.

Butterfly 1 & Moth 1: We both have a four-stage life cycle.

Butterfly 2 & Moth 2: Our first stage is an egg,

Butterfly 3 & Moth 3: then a larva,

Butterfly 4 & Moth 4: a pupa,

Butterfly 5 & Moth 5: and finally an adult.

Butterflies and Moths *(cont.)*

Butterfly 6:   During my pupa state, I did not spin a cocoon. I was hanging unprotected on a branch in a chrysalis.

Moth 6:   During my pupa stage, I did spin a cocoon around my chrysalis for protection.

All Butterflies: We are the butterflies.

All Moths: We are the moths.

All: We are the same, but we are very different!

Note: There are exceptions to each of the differences noted in this script. The facts stated here are the general differences between butterflies and moths.

Performance Note: If using this in a performance, it is fun to dress the butterflies in brightly colored T-shirts and the moths in grays and browns. They could also simply wear tags in the shapes of brightly colored butterflies and dull-colored moths. This would help the audience see the differences between butterflies and moths.

I Love Sixpence

A reader's theater script for six voices

All: I love sixpence, pretty little sixpence.
I love sixpence better than my life!

Reader 1: I spent a penny of it;

Reader 2: I lent a penny of it,

Readers 3–6: And I took fourpence home to my wife.
Oh, my little fourpence, pretty little fourpence.
I love fourpence better than my life!

Reader 3: I spent a penny of it;

Reader 4: I lent a penny of it,

Readers 5–6: And I took twopence home to my wife.
Oh, my little twopence, pretty little twopence.
I love twopence better than my life!

Reader 5: I spent a penny of it;

Reader 6: I lent a penny of it,

Readers 1–4: (*whispered*) And took nothing home to my wife.

All: (*whispered*) Oh, my little nothing, my pretty little nothing
What will nothing buy for my wife?
I have nothing; I spend nothing,
I love nothing better than my wife.

If You See a Fairy Ring

Unknown Author
A reader's theater script for four voices

Reader 1:   If you see a fairy ring

Reader 2:   In a field of grass,

Reader 3:   Very lightly step around,

Reader 4:   Tiptoe as you pass.

Readers 1 & 2:   Last night fairies frolicked there,

Readers 3 & 4:   And they're sleeping somewhere near.

Reader 1:   If you see a tiny fairy

Reader 2:   Lying fast asleep,

Reader 3:   Shut your eyes

Reader 4:   And run away—

Readers 1 & 3:   Do not stay to peek!

Readers 2 & 4:   Do not tell

ALL: Or you'll break a fairy spell!

Performance Note: This script should be performed with very whispery, tentative voices as if the performers were creeping around on tiptoes while speaking.

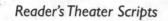

Limericks

A reader's theater script for six voices

Reader 1:   Limericks are special kinds of poems.

Reader 2:   They have five lines.

Reader 1:   The first, second, and fifth lines are longer and end with rhyming words.

Reader 2:   The third and fourth lines rhyme in a different way.

Readers 1 & 2:   Enjoy our limericks and listen for the rhymes.

Reader 3:   There once was a young boy named Clark,

Reader 4:   Who whistled as he walked to the ballpark.

Reader 3:   He had quite a strong arm,

Reader 4:   From his days on the farm,

Readers 3 & 4:   And he pitched the ball almost to Denmark.

Reader 5:   There once was a young girl named Lori,

Reader 6:   Who liked hearing great bedtime stories.

Reader 5:   They would start sounding sad,

Reader 6:   And then turn into glad.

Readers 5 & 6:   She could sleep thinking all's hunky-dory.

Occupational Alphabet

A reader's theater script for 13 voices

Reader 1:   A was an archer who shot at a frog.

Reader 2:   B was a butcher who had a big dog.

All: An archer, a butcher who had a big dog.

Reader 3:   C was a captain with a collar of lace.

Reader 4:   D was a drummer who had a red face.

All: A captain, a drummer who had a red face.

Reader 5:   E was an esquire with pride on his brow.

Reader 6:   F was a farmer who followed his plow.

All: An esquire, a farmer who followed his plow.

Reader 7:   G was a gambler who just had bad luck.

Reader 8:   H was a hunter who hunted a buck.

All: A gambler, a hunter who hunted a buck.

Occupational Alphabet (cont.)

Reader 9: I was an innkeeper who loved to carouse.

Reader 10: J was a joiner who built a big house.

All: An innkeeper, a joiner who built a big house.

Reader 11: K was a king so mighty and grand.

Reader 12: L was a lady who had soft hands.

All: A king, a lady who had soft hands.

Reader 13: M was a miser who hoarded gold.

Reader 1: N was a nobleman, gallant and bold.

All: A miser, a nobleman, gallant and bold.

Reader 2: O was an oyster wench who went about town.

Reader 3: P was a parson wearing a black gown.

All: An oyster, a parson wearing a black gown.

Reader 4: Q was a queen who was fond of good flip.

Reader 5: R was a robber who had a long whip.

All: A queen, a robber who had a long whip.

Occupational Alphabet *(cont.)*

Reader 6:   S was a sailor who spent all he got.

Reader 7:   T was a tinker who mended a pot.

All: A sailor, a tinker who mended a pot.

Reader 8:   U was an upstairs maid who spied an elf.

Reader 9:   V was a vet who worked by himself.

All: A maid, a vet who worked by himself.

Reader 10:   W was a watchman who guarded the door.

Reader 11:   X was expensive and soon became poor.

All: A watchman, expensive who soon became poor.

Reader 12:   Y was a youth who did not love school.

Reader 13:   Z was a zany, poor, harmless fool.

All: A youth, a zany, poor, harmless fool.

Note: This old ABC poem works well with an Early America unit discussing jobs of long ago. To extend this learning, it would be fun to brainstorm a modern-day list of alphabetically arranged jobs. The children could work on rhyming couplets for job descriptions and then put them together for another reader's theater similar to this one. An original modern version of this poem is included in this book on page 73.

Ode to a Prune

A silly reader's theater for many voices: two readers and a chorus

Chorus: Hail to thee, oh prune,
You are never respected.
Hail to thee, oh prune,
I'm not sure just what you expected!

Reader 1: No matter how young a prune may be,
He's always getting wrinkles.

Reader 2: A baby prune is like his dad,
But he's not wrinkled half so bad.

Both: We have wrinkles on our face,
But Pruney has them every place.

Chorus: Hail to thee, oh prune,
You are never respected.
Hail to thee, oh prune,
I'm not sure just what you expected!

Reader 1: No matter how young a prune may be,
He's always getting stewed.

Ode to a Prune (cont.)

Reader 2: Little seed inside the prune,
Is it night or is it noon?

Both : No matter how young a prune may be,
He's always getting wrinkles.

Chorus: Hail to thee, oh prune,
You are never respected.
Hail to thee, oh prune,
I'm not sure just what you expected!

Over in the Meadow

by Olive Wordsworth
A reader's theater script for 10 voices

Reader 1:   Over in the meadow,
                       In the sand in the sun,
                       Lived an old mother toadie
                       And her little toadie one.

Reader 2:   "Wink!" said the mother;

Reader 3:   "I wink!" said the one,

Reader 1:   So they winked and they blinked
                       In the sand in the sun.

Reader 2:   Over in the meadow,
                       Where the stream runs blue,
                       Lived an old mother fish
                       And her little fishes two.

Reader 3:   "Swim!" said the mother;

Readers 4 & 5:   "We swim!" said the two,

Reader 2:   So they swam and they leaped
                       Where the stream runs blue.

Over in the Meadow (cont.)

Reader 3:	Over in the meadow, In a hole in a tree, Lived an old mother bluebird And her little birdies three.
Reader 4:	"Sing!" said the mother;
Readers 5–7:	"We sing!" said the three,
Reader 3:	So they sang and were glad
Reader 4:	In a hole in the tree.
Reader 5:	Over in the meadow, In the reeds on the shore, Lived an old mother muskrat And her little ratties four.
Reader 6:	"Dive!" said the mother;
Readers 6–9:	"We dive!" said the four,
Reader 4:	So they dived and they burrowed In the reeds on the shore.

Over in the Meadow (cont.)

Reader 5: Over in the meadow,
In a snug beehive,
Lived a mother honeybee
And her little bees five.

Reader 6: "Buzz!" said the mother;

Readers 6–10: "We buzz!" said the five,

Reader 5: So they buzzed and they hummed
In the snug beehive.

Reader 6: Over in the meadow,
In a nest built of sticks,
Lived a black mother crow
And her little crows six.

Reader 7: "Caw!" said the mother;

**Readers
8–10 & 1–3:** "We caw!" said the six,

Reader 6: So they cawed and they called
In their nest built of sticks.

Over in the Meadow (cont.)

Reader 7:   Over in the meadow,
Where the grass is so even,
Lived a cheery mother cricket
And her little crickets seven.

Reader 8:   "Chirp!" said the mother;

Readers 9–10 & 1–5: "We chirp!" said the seven,

Reader 7:   So they chirped cheery notes
In the grass soft and even.

Reader 8:   Over in the meadow,
By the old mossy gate,
Lived a brown mother lizard
And her little lizards eight.

Reader 9:   "Bask!" said the mother;

Readers 10, 1–7:   "We bask!" said the eight,

Reader 8:   So they basked in the sun
On the old mossy gate.

Over in the Meadow *(cont.)*

Reader 9:   Over in the meadow,
Where the quiet pools shine,
Lived a green mother frog
And her little froggies nine.

Reader 10:   "Croak!" said the mother;

Readers 1–9:   "We croak!" said the nine,

Reader 9:   So they croaked and they splashed
Where the quiet pools shine.

Reader 10:   Over in the meadow,
In a sly little den,
Lived a gray mother spider
And her little spiders ten.

Reader 1:   "Spin!" said the mother;

All: "We spin!" said the ten,

Reader 10:   So they spun lacy webs
In their sly little den.

The Pledge of Allegiance

A reader's theater script for performance for many voices: the audience and 20 students

Reader 1: (*To the audience*) Let's stand and say the pledge together.

Readers and Audience: I pledge allegiance to the flag of the United States of America. And to the republic for which it stands, one nation, under God, indivisible, with liberty and justice for all.

Reader 1: (*To the audience*) You may be seated.

Reader 2: Kids have been saying the Pledge of Allegiance in school since Columbus Day, 1892.

Reader 3: Since we were in kindergarten, we have been pledging to the American flag each morning.

Reader 4: But this year, we have learned what it means.

All Readers: I pledge…

Reader 5: The word pledge means to promise!

All Readers: I pledge allegiance…

The Pledge of Allegiance (cont.)

Reader 6: The word allegiance means to be loyal and supportive.

All Readers: I pledge allegiance to the flag of the United States of America.

Reader 7: A flag is a special piece of cloth with a certain design and colors.

Reader 8: A flag is used to represent a state or country.

Reader 9: Our American flag is sometimes called Old Glory

Reader 10: or The Stars and Stripes.

Reader 11: The flag has 13 equal stripes of red and white.

Reader 12: The stripes represent the 13 original colonies.

Reader 13: It also has 50 white five-pointed stars on a blue rectangle.

Reader 14: The stars represent the 50 states today.

All Readers: I pledge allegiance to the flag of the United States of America. And to the republic for which it stands...

Reader 15: A *republic* is a country that allows the citizens, or the people who live there, to choose their own leaders.

Reader 16: Those leaders are representatives,

The Pledge of Allegiance *(cont.)*

Reader 17: senators,

Reader 18: and even our president.

All Readers: I pledge allegiance to the flag of the United States of America. And to the republic for which it stands, one nation...

Reader 19: "One nation" is an important fact about our country.

Reader 20: Even though we have 50 different states,

Reader 1: from Alaska to Florida and from Maine to Hawaii,

Reader 2: we are all united under one government in Washington, D.C.

All Readers: I pledge allegiance to the flag of the United States of America. And to the republic for which it stands, one nation, under God...

Reader 3: In the original pledge, the phrase "under God" was not included.

Reader 4: But in 1954, Dwight Eisenhower was our president.

Reader 5: He added the new phrase "under God" to our pledge.

The Pledge of Allegiance (cont.)

Reader 6: It was taken from Abraham Lincoln's Gettysburg Address where he says, "That this nation, under God."

All: I pledge allegiance to the flag of the United States of America. And to the republic for which it stands, one nation, under God, indivisible...

Reader 7: Indivisible means you cannot divide the United States into parts.

Reader 8: From 1861 to 1865, our country was divided.

Reader 9: The Civil War divided the United States into the North and the South.

Reader 10: Our pledge has us promise to stay united,

Reader 11: never dividing again.

All: I pledge allegiance to the flag of the United States of America. And to the republic for which it stands, one nation, under God, indivisible, with liberty...

Reader 12: *Liberty* simply means freedom.

Reader 13: Americans have the freedom to think the way they want.

The Pledge of Allegiance (cont.)

Reader 14:   And they can express their opinions out loud.

All: I pledge allegiance to the flag of the United States of America. And to the republic for which it stands, one nation, under God, indivisible, with liberty and justice for all.

Reader 15:   "Justice for all" means that our laws will be fair for everyone.

Reader 16:   Every American deserves to be treated fairly and with respect.

Readers 17 & 18:   And that is the meaning of the Pledge of Allegiance.

Readers 19 & 20:   Let's all stand and say it one more time.

All: I pledge allegiance to the flag of the United States of America. And to the republic for which it stands, one nation, under God, indivisible, with liberty and justice for all.

President Lincoln, I've Been Thinkin'

A reader's theater for five voices: four readers and Abraham Lincoln

Reader 1: President Lincoln, I've been thinkin'
When you were a tiny babe.
As a youth you told the truth,
So people called you Honest Abe.

All: Honest Abe!
Honest Abe!
People called you Honest Abe.

Reader 2: President Lincoln, I've been thinkin'
You grew up as tough as nails.
On the farm, you swung your arm,
And with an axe, you split the rails!

All: Split the rails!
Split the rails!
With an axe, you split the rails!

President Lincoln, I've Been Thinkin' *(cont.)*

Reader 3: President Lincoln, I've been thinkin'
How you taught yourself the law.
Every book around, you took,
And read like no one ever saw!

All: Ever saw!
Ever saw!
And read like no one ever saw!

Reader 4: President Lincoln, I've been thinkin'
Back to when you wrote the
Emancipation Proclamation
So the slaves could all be free.

All: All be free!
All be free!
So the slaves could all be free!

President Lincoln, I've Been Thinkin' *(cont.)*

Lincoln:	"A house divided against itself cannot stand. I believe this government cannot endure, permanently half slave and half free. I do not expect the Union to be dissolved—I do not expect the house to fall—but I do expect it will cease to be divided. It will become all one thing or all the other."
All:	President Lincoln, we've been thinkin' How you bravely led the land. Once divided, now united, You made sure our house would stand! Our house would stand! Our house would stand! You made sure our house would stand!

Note: The inserted speech by Abraham Lincoln is from 1858, before he became president. Even then, he knew that the United States was headed for a crisis that later became the Civil War.

Performance Note: The performance is especially effective if Lincoln stands in the middle wearing a stovepipe hat for identification. The readers can then direct their voices at Lincoln.

The Battle Within:
An Old Cherokee Conversation

*A reader's theater for four voices: two narrators, a
Cherokee grandfather, and his grandson*

Narrator 1:   On a cold evening, an old Cherokee man sat at a fire with his grandson.

Narrator 2:   He was talking about battles of years gone by.

Narrator 1:   But then his attention turned to the battle that goes on within every human being— the battle within.

Narrator 2:   His grandson asked,

Grandson: "How can there be a battle inside of someone?"

Narrator 2:   The grandfather replied,

Grandfather: "My son, the battle is between two wolves inside us all. One is Evil. It is anger, envy, jealousy, sorrow, regret, greed, arrogance, self-pity, guilt, and resentment."

The Battle Within:
An Old Cherokee Conversation *(cont.)*

Narrator 1: The grandson listened intently to his grandfather.

Narrator 2: The grandfather continued.

Grandfather: "The other is Good. It is joy, peace, love, hope, serenity, humility, kindness, benevolence, empathy, generosity, truth, compassion, and faith."

Narrator 2: The grandson thought about it for a moment, and then he asked,

Grandson: "Which wolf wins."

Narrator 1: The wise grandfather replied,

Grandfather: "The one you feed."

Performance Note: When practicing this script, it is very important for the grandfather to take his time in describing Good and Evil. He is a very wise man. He should pause thoughtfully between each descriptive word separated by a comma.

The Hayloft

Poem by Robert Louis Stevenson

A reader's theater for four voices

Reader 1:   Through all the pleasant meadow-side,
the grass grew shoulder-high;

Reader 2:   Till the shining scythes went far and wide
and cut it down to dry.

Reader 3:   These green and sweetly smelling crops
they led in wagons home;

Reader 4:   And they piled them here in mountaintops
for mountaineers to roam.

Reader 1:   Here is Mount Clear,

Reader 2:   Mount Rusty Nail,

Reader 3:   Mount Eagle,

Reader 4:   and Mount High—

Reader 1:   The mice that in these mountains dwell,
no happier than I!

Reader 2:   O what a joy to clamber there,

Reader 3:   O what a place for play!

Reader 4:   With the sweet, the dim, the dusty air—

All: The happy hills of hay!

 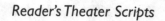

The Nail

An old story retold by Lorraine Griffith

*A reader's theater for nine voices: six narrators,
two stable boys, and a tradesman*

Narrator 1:   A long, long time ago, there was a man who traded goods for a living.

Narrator 2:   He had just finished a big morning of trading at a local fair.

Narrator 3:   His bags were full of gold and silver.

Narrator 4:   He strapped the bags on his horse's back and left for home.

Narrator 5:   After a few hours of travel, he stopped at a stable to water his horse.

Narrator 6:   A stable boy said to him,

Stable Boy 1:   "Sir, a nail is missing in the shoe of your horse. It is the left-hind foot."

Narrator 1:   The tradesman was in a hurry to get home, so he simply ignored the boy's warning.

Tradesman: "It will be okay!"

The Nail *(cont.)*

Narrator 2:   he yelled as he galloped away down the road.

Narrator 3:   Later in the day, the man stopped again.

Narrator 4:   Another stable boy was concerned about the horse.

Stable Boy 2:   "May I take your horse to a farrier? He is missing a nail in his left-hind shoe."

Narrator 5:   Again the tradesman was in a hurry to get home, so he simply ignored the boy's warning.

Tradesman: "It will be okay!"

Narrator 6:   he yelled as he galloped away down the road.

Narrator 1:   Still a few hours from home, the horse began to limp.

Narrator 2:   But still the tradesman was in a hurry and stayed on the horse.

Narrator 3:   Then the horse began to stumble.

Narrator 4:   But still the tradesman was in a hurry and stayed on the horse.

The Nail *(cont.)*

Narrator 5: Finally the horse fell and broke his leg.

Narrator 6: The tradesman couldn't believe it—

Narrator 1: here he was on the dark road at early evening

Narrator 2: and he had no horse to take him home.

Narrator 3: Sadly, he had to leave his injured horse there on the road.

Narrator 4: He had to carry the heavy bags of silver and gold all the way home.

Narrators 5 & 6: And all the way home, he kept thinking,

Tradesman: "If only I had taken care of my horse and had that one nail replaced. I was in a hurry. All of my problems are because of this nail."

Stable Boys: Sometimes the faster you go, the slower you are!

The Nail: A New Version

A reader's theater script for nine voices: six narrators, a man, a clerk, and a woman

Narrator 1: Just last week, a man was on his way home from a business trip.

Narrator 2: It was pretty late at night, and he needed to wake up from the hum of the road.

Narrator 3: He was about three hours from home.

Narrator 4: He pulled off the interstate to spend a little time at an electronics store.

Narrator 5: He was looking for a new part for his computer!

Narrator 6: Well, instead of finding the computer part,

Narrator 1: he found a

Narrator 2: brand new,

Narrator 3: high-definition,

Narrator 4: wide-screen television!

Man: It was on sale!

Narrator 5: The box was huge, but just fit in his brand new pickup truck.

Narrator 6: As he was leaving the parking lot, the clerk yelled,

The Nail: A New Version (cont.)

Clerk: "Hey! I think there is a nail in your tire!"

Man: "It'll be okay! I just have a few hours to go!"

Narrator 1: Just before he made it to the interstate for the three-hour ride home,

Narrator 5: he stopped for a cup of coffee at the local coffeehouse.

Narrator 6: As he drove off, a woman in the parking lot flagged him down!

Woman: "Hey! I think there is a nail in your tire!"

Man: "It'll be okay! I just have a few hours to go!"

Narrator 1: The man couldn't wait to get the truck up to 70 miles per hour, and get on home with his

Narrator 2: brand new,

Narrator 3: high-definition,

Narrator 4: wide-screen television!

Man: After all, it was on sale!

Narrator 5: As soon as the speedometer hit 70,

The Nail: A New Version *(cont.)*

Narrator 6: the man felt a bit of a strange sensation in the truck.

Narrator 1: Then he heard a flopping sound and he knew it!

Clerk & Woman: His tire was flat!

Narrator 2: But by the time he could slow down,

Narrator 3: not only was his tire flat,

Narrator 4: but the rim was bent!

Narrator 5: The man was great with computers but not with changing a tire!

Narrator 6: And to make matters worse, he had forgotten to renew his auto membership!

Narrator 1: And even if he had someone to call, he had forgotten to recharge his cell phone.

Narrator 5: Sadly, because of the huge

Narrator 2: brand new,

Narrator 3: high-definition,

Narrator 4: wide-screen television

The Nail: A New Version (cont.)

Narrator 6: in the back of the truck,

Narrator 1: the man could only sit in the back with the television

Narrator 2: and hope for daylight.

Narrator 3: As he sat with his only friend, the television, he thought,

Man: "If only I had taken care of my tire and had that one nail pulled out. I was in a hurry. All of my problems are because of that one nail!

Clerk & Woman: Sometimes the faster you go, the slower you are!

The Sentence Team

A reader's theater script for four voices: a noun, a verb, an adjective, and an adverb.

Noun: I am a noun.

Verb: I am a verb.

Adjective: I am an adjective.

Adverb: I am an adverb.

All: We are all parts of speech. But each of us has a different job in a sentence.

Noun: I name a person, place, or thing.
I am all about teachers, schools, and pizza.

Verb: I am action words!
I am all about jumping, running, and singing.

Adjective: I am a noun's best friend, because I describe nouns, like pizza. I use words like spicy, hot, and delicious.

Adverb: I am a verb's best friend, because I describe verbs, like jumping. I use words like quickly, recklessly, and energetically.

The Sentence Team *(cont.)*

All: We are all very important words. Just listen to how we work together to make a great sentence!

Adjective: Happy

Noun: children

Verb: run

Adverb: freely.

Adverb & Adjective: (*Looking at each other*) Wow! Look how important we are! Without us, the sentence would be boring!

Noun: (*Boring tone*) Children

Verb: (*Boring tone*) run.

Adverb & Adjective: (*Looking at each other again*) Let's use our power and change the sentence completely!

Adjective: Tired

Noun: children

Verb: run

Adverb: lazily.

The Sentence Team *(cont.)*

Noun & Verb: Wow! You two are magical!

All: Let's try another one!

Noun: Sandy

Verb: loves

Adjective: hot, crusty

Noun: pizza.

Adverb: Hey wait a minute! I feel left out!!

Verb, Adjective, & Noun: Sorry!

Noun: Sandy

Adverb: really

Verb: loves

Adjective: hot, crusty

Noun: pizza.

All: And that is how we work together! Each of us is important, but we work together as a team. Just call us the Sentence Team!

The Sparrow's Nest

Poem by Mary Howitt
A reader's theater script for seven voices

Reader 1:   Just look what I have found!

Reader 2:   A Sparrow's nest upon the ground;

Reader 3:   A Sparrow's nest as you may see, blown out of yonder old elm tree.

Reader 4:   And what a medley thing it is!

Reader 5:   I never saw a nest like this;

Reader 6:   Not neatly wove with decent care of silvery moss and shining hair.

Reader 7:   But put together, odds and ends, picked up from enemies and friends;

Reader 4:   See, bits of thread, and bits of rag, just like a little rubbish-bag!

Reader 5:   Here is a scrap of red and brown, like the old washer-woman's gown;

Reader 1:   And here is muslin, pink and green,

The Sparrow's Nest (cont.)

Reader 2:   And bits of calico between.

Reader 3:   See, hair of dog and fur of cat,

Reader 6:   And rovings of a worsted mat;

Reader 7:   And threads of silks,

Reader 2:   and many a feather,

Reader 1:   Compacted cunningly together.

Reader 3:   Had these odds and ends been brought to some wise man renowned for thought,

Reader 4:   Some man

Reader 5:   —of men a very gem—

Reader 4:   Pray, what could he have done with them?

All: If we had said,

Reader 7:   "Here, sir, we bring you many a worthless little thing;

Reader 6:   Just bits and scraps, so very small, that they have scarcely size at all.

Reader 1:   And out of these, you must contrive a dwelling large enough for five;

The Sparrow's Nest *(cont.)*

Reader 2: Neat, warm, and snug with comfort stored for five small things to lodge and board."

Reader 3: How would the man of learning vast, have been astonished and aghast;

Reader 5: And vowed that such a thing had been ne'er heard of,

Reader 4: thought of,

All: much less seen!

Performance Note: This poem is full of wonder! The performance of this text should reflect how amazing it is that a sparrow could use so many scattered materials to create such a warm and perfect nest for five baby birds.

There Was

Poems by Edward Lear
A reader's theater script for six voices: two narrators and four readers

Narrator 1: Edward Lear was a poet who wrote humorous limericks and nonsense poetry.

Narrator 2: Sometimes it's hard to imagine people who were funny in the days of long ago.

Narrator 1: And Edward Lear lived long ago, almost 200 years ago.

Narrator 2: With us today are four readers who are each going to read aloud one of Lear's most famous limericks.

Reader 1: There was an old person whose habits
induced him to feed upon rabbits;

Narrators: He fed upon rabbits?
What a strange habit!

Reader 1: When he'd eaten eighteen,
He turned perfectly green—
Upon which he relinquished those habits!

Reader 2: There was a young lady whose nose
Continually prospers and grows;

Narrators: It prospers and grows?
A young lady's nose?

There Was *(cont.)*

Reader 2:   When it grew out of sight,
She exclaimed in a fright,
"Oh! Farewell to the end of my nose!"

Reader 3:   There was an old man with a beard
Who said, "It is just as I feared!"

Narrators: This man with a beard,
What is it he feared?

Reader 3:   "Two owls and a hen,
Four larks and a wren
Have all built their nests in my beard!"

Reader 4:   There was a young lady of Niger
Who smiled as she rode on a tiger;

Narrators: If you were from Niger,
Would you ride on a tiger?

Reader 4:   They returned from the ride
With the lady inside,
And a smile on the face of the tiger.

Performance Note: When the narrators are listening to the limericks, they are making comments to each other about the silliness of the first two lines. This arrangement is an effort for children to think about the silliness of nonsense poems.

The Fairies

Poem by William Allingham
A reader's theater for six voices

Reader 1:   Up the airy mountain,

Reader 2:   down the rushy glen,

Readers
1 & 2:   We daren't go a-hunting for fear of little men.

Reader 3:   Wee folk,

Reader 4:   good folk

Readers
3 & 4:   trooping all together;

Reader 5:   Green jacket,

Reader 6:   red cap,

Readers
5 & 6:   and white owl's feather!

Reader 1:   Down along the rocky shore, some make their home.

Reader 2:   They live on crispy pancakes of yellow tide-foam;

Reader 3:   Some in the reeds of the black mountain lake,

Readers
1–3:   With frogs for their watch-dogs all night awake.

Reader 4:   By the craggy hillside through the mosses bare,

The Fairies *(cont.)*

Reader 5: They have planted thorn trees for pleasure here and there.

Reader 6: If any man is so daring as dig them up in spite,

Reader 4–6: He shall find the sharpest thorns in his bed at night.

Reader 1: Up the airy mountain,

Reader 2: down the rushy glen,

Readers 1 & 2: We daren't go a-hunting for fear of little men.

Reader 3: Wee folk,

Reader 4: good folk

Readers 3 & 4: trooping all together;

Reader 5: Green jacket,

Reader 6: red cap,

Readers 5 & 6: and white owl's feather!

The Old Man Learns a Lesson

A reader's theater script for five voices: four narrators and an old woman

Narrator 1: There was an old man who lived in a wood,
As you may plainly see;

Narrator 2: He said he could do as much work in a day
As his wife could do in three.

Old Woman: "With all my heart,"

Narrator 3: the old woman said,

Old Woman: "If you will allow;
Tomorrow you'll stay at home in my stead,
And I'll go drive the plow.

But you must milk Bessie, the cow,
For fear that she'll go dry;
And you must feed the little pigs
That are within the sty.

And you must mind the speckled hen,
For fear she'll lay astray;
And you must reel the spool of yarn
That I spun yesterday."

The Old Man Learns a Lesson <small>(cont.)</small>

Narrator 4:   The old woman took a staff in her hand,
And went to drive the plow;

Narrator 1:   The old man took a pail in his hand
And went to milk the cow.

Narrator 2:   But Bessie flinched and Bessie hinched,
And Bessie broke his nose;

Narrator 3:   Then Tidy gave him such a blow
That the blood ran down to his toes.

Narrator 4:   He went to feed the little pigs,
That were within the sty;

Narrator 1:   He hit his head against a beam,
And it made the blood to fly.

Narrator 2:   He went to mind the speckled hen,
For fear she'd lay astray;

Narrator 3:   And he forgot the spool of yarn
His wife spun yesterday.

Narrator 4:   So he swore by the sun, the moon, and the stars,
And the green leaves on the tree;

Narrator 1:   If his wife didn't do a day's work in her life

All: She should never be ruled by he.

Works Cited

Chard, D.J., S. Vaughn, and B. Tyler. (2002). A synthesis of research on effective interventions for building fluency with elementary students with learning disabilities. *Journal of Learning Disabilities*, 35, 386–406.

Dowhower, S. L. (1987). Effects of repeated reading on second-grade transitional readers' fluency and comprehension. *Reading Research Quarterly*, 22, 389–407.

Dowhower, S. L. (1994). Repeated reading revisited: Research into practice. *Reading and Writing Quarterly*, 10, 343–358.

Griffith, L. W., & T.V. Rasinski. (2004). A focus on fluency: How one teacher incorporated fluency with her reading curriculum. The Reading Teacher, 58, 126–137.

Kuhn, M.R., & S.A. Stahl. (2000). Fluency: A review of developmental and remedial practices (CIERA Rep. No. 2–008). Ann Arbor, MI: Center for the Improvement of Early Reading Achievement.

Rasinski, T.V. (2003). *The fluent reader: Oral reading strategies for building word recognition, fluency, and comprehension.* New York: Scholastic.

Rasinski, T.V. (2006). Reading fluency instruction: Moving beyond accuracy, automaticity, and prosody. *The Reading Teacher*, 59, 704–706.

Rasinski, T.V. (in press). Teaching reading fluency artfully: A professional and personal journey. In R. Fink and S. J. Samules (editors), *Inspiring Reading Success: Interest and Motivation in an Age of High-Stakes Testing.* Newark, DE: International Reading Association.

Rasinski, T.V., & J.V. Hoffman. (2003). Theory and research into practice: Oral reading in the school literacy curriculum. Reading Research Quarterly, 38, 510–522.

Samuels, S. J. (1979). The method of repeated readings. *The Reading Teacher*, 32, 403–408. Also, in *The Reading Teacher*, (1997, February), page 376+.

Index